6 Short Stories:
Learn Tarot in a Day

Ian Eshey

ISBN-13: 978-1-4936-0157-8
ISBN-10: 1-4936-0157-1

Contents

Chapter 4: Suite of Cups Represents Love and Emotions ... page 37

Advice on Love and Relationships
The Story No.3: Fulfillment of the Cups
Here's How to Memorize the Cups Cards

Chapter 5: Wands Suite Represents Your Passion and Drive ... page 41

A Powerful Force but Hard to Control
The Story No.4: Implementation of the Wands
Here's How to Memorize the Wands Cards

Chapter 6: Pentacles Suite Represents Money and Material Matters ... page 45

Material World: Get Down to Earth
The Story No.5: The Hard Work of the Pentacles
Here's How to Memorize the Pentacles Cards

Chapter 7: Court Cards Represent Different Personalities and the Actual People ... page 49

Tricky to Learn but Easy to Recognize
The Story No.6: Discussion of the Court Cards
Here's How to Memorize the Court Cards

Chapter 8: The Lazy Man's Way to Perform Complete Tarot Readings ... page 59

Chapter 9: Putting it All Together – Examples of Real-Life Tarot Readings ... page 65

Thank You for Reading ... page 85

Foreword

Tarot is my hobby and it is best to make it clear up front – I'm not an expert. I just enjoy it tremendously for a decade now, and I'll share with you the way to make sense out of Tarot (and quickly) in the same way I discovered it.

Note that this book is not meant to be the ultimate resource you'll need to learn all the depths of Tarot cards' meanings or to address all the intricacies of performing live Tarot readings.

Its goal is somewhat different: This book's purpose is to help you learn much, much faster.

Later today when you have finished this book, you will be able to start performing tarot readings all by yourself.

You don't believe me? Please drop me an email in a few hours and tell me what you think by then. Contact information is at the end of the book.

The method described in the following chapters came to me seemingly by accident. I have used that method myself, to feel like the fog has suddenly lifted.

And at the time I'm writing this foreword to the second edition (Summer 2013), thousands of people have used this same method after purchasing this book via Amazon and others. A great majority of the feedback being unanimously positive and repeating such terms as "simple" and "refreshing".

Any critique was mainly targeted at lacking the traditional rich (and for the "uninitiated" folks mostly quite mystifying) card-by-card in-depth explanations.

At first it seemed weird to me, since the whole point of this book is precisely to avoid that "take one card each day and write down everything that comes to your mind" mentality. (And to avoid the 78 days required to implement that otherwise sound advice.)

But some people perhaps purchased a Tarot deck with no book included in the package. Or they felt that any Tarot learning book without such information was incomplete. And to be frank, exploring the richness of Tarot from such detailed book can be great fun and a reward all by itself.

Adding such material in this book seemed counter-productive since my initial goal and much of my effort was to keep this book as short as possible to make it quick to read.

So I decided to add a separate book for free; a companion for this one you hold in your hands right now. This companion book presents exactly such classic view on the cards and it has almost 100 pages btw.

Get the free companion e-book with traditional all-cards explanations via download link in Major Arcana chapter.

Ok, let's begin with what you came here for – learning Tarot. In the next chapter I'll give you some surprisingly simple explanations that will cut your learning time dramatically.

Chapter 1.
Grasp Tarot Basics in
15 Minutes or Less

You Ask a Question and Your
Subconscious Does the Rest

For centuries, Tarot has meant different things to different people. For me, it's a source of advice: a fun and insightful mechanism of consulting one's own subconscious resources, very much like the ancient I-Ch'ing of the Chinese.

When I need to think about a real life situation I have gotten myself into, consulting a Tarot always provides me with fresh insights. The fact is my subconscious has already dwelt on the problem. So Tarot reading is a great way to let my deeper mind point me to some crucial detail or new angle to consider.

So far so good, but how does reading for other people work?

Because Tarot is a mechanism for contacting the subconscious, if you read cards for someone else you simply must explore the situation together. There's no other way.

You shouldn't just spread the cards for someone and construct a nice story all by yourself while the other person keeps her mouth shut. That's only contacting your intuition instead of paying careful attention to hers.

Professional "fortune tellers" might just seem to pull everything they say solely out of the cards; or out of the hat, sometimes. But in reality they are extremely perceptive to reactions of the querent (the person for whom they are reading the cards), whether consciously or not.

And while we are talking about fortune telling, can Tarot really see the future?

I personally don't try to predict the future but our subconscious surely knows better than our rational (and utterly biased) mind the most probable outcome of some complicated situation we are in – if we don't take a different approach this time.

On the other hand, predicting that you will run into someone two and a half months from now and get married next year, to raise a beautiful little girl who will become a ballet dancer – is really stretching it too far. It's pure entertainment, at best.

So how do you actually do that "consulting" with your inner self? I'll show you in a moment.

How to Listen and Start Getting Answers

People with a healthy amount of skepticism immediately point out that advice from the cards is pretty universal and can be applied to most people in most situations.

But until they stop and think about it, they don't see one pretty obvious thing. For two completely different people in completely different situations, exactly the same card will bring to the surface completely different associations.

This is why every single Tarot book or article tells you that the most important "trick" of all is to let your intuition guide you.

Fortunately, most "modern" (the last hundred years or so) Tarot decks are illustrated and rich with symbolism; which is not accidental. In simple words, pay attention to what catches your eye on a particular card; that's your intuition; it has just signaled something to you!

For example, let's say that the Moon on a particular card in a reading somehow "feels" important. That feeling comes from somewhere deep inside YOU, not from the card itself. This means that it's your own subconscious, telling you to rely more on your intuition, but to be wary of mistaking illusions for reality. This is what the Moon basically represents.

And don't worry. I'll get to basics of Tarot symbolism, along with most common symbols, later in this chapter.

Let's take a look at another example. You are contemplating a particular career situation, but most cards in a spread are Cups. And Cups usually represent emotions. What does that mean?

If your subconscious disregards it, then it probably means nothing. But if your intuition is sounding a clear alarm here, then obviously you should focus on the emotions involved between the parties. Never mind it's business you are analyzing, your intuition has just told you what to look for.

The Secret of Why Tarot Cards are Beautiful

People have always given much thought to the deeper meaning of the things that surround us. Tarot uses that deeply rooted symbolism heavily. And it's a good thing, for one simple reason: You already KNOW the "hidden" implications of most of those symbols!

How can that be? The answer is simple. Those same symbols are part of every culture on Earth. The Sun is good; night is dangerous and so on.

Here I'll summarize the most common symbols and what they usually represent; don't try to memorize the whole thing. After simply reading through it, you will be able to easily develop further associations yourself; which is much more important.

Let's start with the symbolic meanings of the four Tarot suits themselves. But first, to summarize them for those of you who are new to Tarot.

Four Tarot Suits

Tarot deck has 22 cards of Major Arcana (more about that later) and four suits: Cups, Wands, Swords and Pentacles. Each suit advises on some segment of everyday life. To keep things simple for now:

Cups represent your emotions; basically your love life and relationships with other people.

Wands represent your spirit; your passions, your drive and your projects.

Swords represent your intellect; in other words your rational mind which in Tarot more often than not leads to open conflict.

Pentacles (or Coins) represent more material things; money, home, your health.

So what are the symbols here?

Cups represent the Water element, which is a life source, the symbol of natural cycles, and rarely acts directly – its actions are indirect but very powerful, and water always finds its way, just like emotions.

Wands are made of wood, which easily turns to raging fire – a powerful force but hard to control.

Swords have two sides of the blades and represent the mind (traditionally associated with the Air element), which solves complex problems but can also be source of conflict and destruction and is to be used carefully.

Pentacles represent the Earth element and symbolize material (more "down to earth") matters, not simply money, and also physical manifestations of stability, caution and effort.

See? Now it's easy to make further connections.

For example, Pentacles in particular situation can draw your attention to generosity or a lack of it, or to the need for good, old-fashioned effort. Or even to being overly cautious and guilty of too much planning and too little action.

People on Tarot cards

Another symbolism is in how people on Tarot cards carry themselves.

People depicted on the cards clearly show their emotions or where their focus is. If they are turning their back, they are usually contemplating something, and if they have blinded eyes, they can't see something obvious to others.

Children and family represent harmony and happiness; or they may picture a moment of rest before things get rolling again.

Pages are naive and hunting for experience while Knights are experienced and action oriented. Queens are mature, wise and subtle; and Kings are mature, knowledgeable and in control.

Females, generally speaking, represent Yin, which represents stability, action through indirect means and relying on intuition. Males represent Yang: they are dynamic and prone to more direct means, like pursuing rational argument or taking direct action.

Astrological Symbols

A Star represents guidance and hope.

The Sun is huge power and positive energy, and brings clear visibility of all things. There are, of course, many more associations we connect with the Sun, but they should be intuitive enough for each and every one of us; for example, the Sun rising after the night or the Sun chasing the clouds away.

The Moon is also a force of nature, representing the cyclical nature of things and our perception relying more on intuition, but under the influence of the Moon sometimes it's not easy to distinguish reality from illusion.

More Common Symbols

Ships often represent starting on a journey, and with the Oceans they sail on, we associate not only unlimited possibilities but also a higher force that we can't influence.

Path is exactly that; but more likely than not, it's not a physical path. Mountains are at the same time obstacles and goals that open new horizons when reached.

Fields and Harvest represent results as well as the connections between actions and their consequences.

The Wall is a limitation and a Castle far away symbolizes stability and the safety we have yet to achieve, like a final or intermediate goal, but nonetheless important.

The Bridge lets you transition from the present (for example, a negative) context and surroundings to another; it is basically the means to get to somewhere else but it needs to be found and used – it cannot do anything by itself.

There are many more, but you get the point. And whatever deck you use, you can bet it will be full of the above symbols and the like.

Now that you understand what the symbols are for, there is in fact only one more thing you absolutely need; basic numerology.

I'm not kidding. With just these two things: understanding the numbers 1 to 10 and paying attention to symbols, you could figure out the meanings of all the four suits' cards for yourself (but there is even easier way which I'll show you later).

So let's get to the meaning of numbers.

Here's a Quick Way to See Progressions in the Cards Right Away

What has numerology to do with Tarot? Simply speaking, each suit's cards, from the Ace (which is One) to Ten, represent progression from a new beginning and great potential (Ace) to a conclusion (Ten). This conclusion is at the same time the base for the next cycle for the theme represented by each of the four Tarot suits.

Ok, **Ones** are beginnings and **Tens** are conclusions; what are the numbers in between?

After the Ace comes the **Two** which represents a choice or decision to be made and also the need for balance or the connection of two inherently separate things.

Three represents first tangible results and situation development.

Four represents stability and solid foundations (e.g. four corners of a house); but it could also indicate increasing boredom as there is a lack of dynamics.

Five ruins the balance and brings unexpected change with all the challenges that go with it.

Six again brings stability in one way or another and things can go on.

Seven brings a moment of rest and the opportunity to plan the next steps, while

Eight puts material stability (e.g. money or something palpable) in focus as either a positive or a negative influence.

Nine represents the last step before coming to a conclusion, with all the consequences of past actions and all the good and the bad associations that come with it. For example, a harvest is associated with finally getting the results of hard work and planning; – there is still work to do, but the conclusion is in sight.

Let's try it. What could the Two of Swords mean?

To make it dead simple, we'll go over it one factor at a time.

Two means decision or need for balance. Swords are intellect and conflict. The picture is usually a pretty tough one depending on what deck you use (two swords in hands of a Valkyrie-like non-smiling war goddess are enough to make anyone pause). Here is the Two of Swords from Rider-Waite Tarot deck:

So it's a tough (just look at the picture) decision (Two) requiring cold analytical thought (Swords); maybe trying to balance (Two) contradicting interests which will probably lead to conflict (Swords). Once a decision is made, there is no going back (picture again).

It wasn't hard at all, was it? We just combined the meaning of the number with the symbols on the picture (including the suit!). And if you have a good deck, the picture will communicate all of that almost by itself.

There is nothing mystical here. In fact, you must admit it's pretty straight-forward. (Don't worry if you like finesse, there will be plenty of it later in the book, especially when we come to actually performing the readings).

This is useful to understand because your mind actually does put such things together pretty quickly. But we don't want you analyzing bits and pieces and putting them back together like in the above example. You need to KNOW the cards so you can focus on the bigger picture.

Now let's see how we'll go about actually teaching you all the cards in the shortest time possible.

How to Actually Learn All 78 Tarot Cards Quickly

Learning the meanings of and nuances for each of 78 cards doesn't sound easy or fun. Especially when you realize that each card can mean many different things depending on the context.

When I was starting with Tarot, I tried to read spreads by simply reading the meanings from a book that came with the deck. You have probably guessed that I was more often than not pretty frustrated with the results.

But the breakthrough came when I realized that each card isn't an independent entity; cards follow each other and describe different stages in real life cycles such as a person maturing, an idea developing, or a project advancing.

Look at Tarot cards as situation progressions!

Moreover, such progressions are easy to tell as a story. To our ancestors, stories were the single main mechanism of passing on information. Our brains are designed to catch a "thread" in a story and automatically attach the details along the way.

Thus, I have written six short stories containing all 78 cards primarily to help myself. These same stories are contained in the following chapters, ready for you to quickly and easily learn the meanings of each card.

One additional benefit is that you will be able to automatically think of each card as part of "progression" (What happened before? What is yet to come?), which is much more powerful than simply considering the meaning of one card in isolation.

Now about learning…

Of course you will learn much quicker if you apply several well-known general rules for learning anything. These as follows (keeping it simple): using different channels, maintaining interest and repetition.

Use Multiple Channels

The different channels of learning are viewing, listening, speaking and doing. Simply combine them as you like, just use more than one channel; read the stories, look at the cards, read aloud, discuss the cards and the readings with friends, or open spreads for yourself. Use your imagination here.

Be Careful to Maintain Your Interest

If you lose interest along the way, it's a sure bet you won't learn much. One of the tricks to maintaining your interest is to define mini goals, for example, "learning" a single story. Or being able to open spreads still using the book you received with your deck, but now with your own understanding kicking in and completing the picture.

Using different channels imaginatively also helps. Try several ways of learning to avoid getting bored, and don't try to do all at once to avoid burnout.

Repeat What You Have Just Learned

After you have read a story, repeat what you have just learned. Then do something else for 15 minutes to let your memory integrate the information, and then repeat once more – and tomorrow again. That's all it takes.

Numerous studies have shown a huge (several times!) difference in memorized information between those who don't practice repeating what they have just "learned" and those who practice in the above mentioned or a similar way.

To summarize, you will use the above learning tips and the very basics that I have explained about Tarot in general to learn the cards – and to make it stick.

Now combine that with the story about Major Arcana from the next chapter and you will memorize the cards in no time.

Chapter 2.
Major Arcana
Represents the Big
Lessons in Life

Maturing and Overcoming Life Challenges

Most tarot decks have 22 major arcana cards, usually beginning with "The Fool" and ending with "The World." Major arcana cards don't belong to any suite and are the heart of a tarot deck. Those special cards don't deal with mundane and everyday worries. Each major arcana card depicts an experience that changes us.

In other words, major arcana are big lessons in life.

Those lessons put together make a natural progression. Everybody goes through this progression while accumulating experience and integrating it into part of him or herself. There are steps we all take, either in the same or similar order. As new situations arise, we first, analyze them with our rational mind, but we mature only when we integrate on an emotional level, everything we have learned.

Sometimes, we talk about Major Arcana as experiences we gather from birth to death. Don't take it too literally. The beginning of major arcana represents the beginning of new cycle in life, and with ending of major arcana, this cycle is complete, but everything is getting ready for new beginning.

This is somewhat like a person graduating on this "plane" and continuing life on higher and more balanced level; more wisely and more fully but with new challenges emerging.

With each challenge, a person matures and gains confidence, as well as understanding of the world. This all works towards the successful completion of the cycle and getting ready for the next journey.

You could say that Major Arcana represents our inner selves, struggling to find our higher purpose.

So when a Major Arcana card shows up in a reading, it requires special attention. Each reading is a story and Major Arcana, if present, is the heart of that story.

I wrote the following story precisely to learn and understand Major Arcana cards. It proved invaluable both for me back then, as for thousands of others in the years since.

The story goes on card-by-card, telling you about a person naive and open to new experiences just starting on the journey. On this path, the person will have many realizations and overcome many challenges coming from the outside world, as well as from the person's own emotions and beliefs.

If you have a deck near you, now would be a good time to use it. No real problem if you don't, but looking at the cards will speed up your learning (multiple channels, remember) and it's fun.

Separate the Major Arcana cards from the deck. As the card comes up in the story, just put it in front of you and pay attention to the image on the card…

Oh, and I have told you I'll give you the link to a (free) companion e-book when we come to learning the cards. Your download link is at the end of this chapter.

The Story No.1: Fools' Journey

You start the journey as a Fool (0), naive and carefree, excited by all the new experiences. In search of knowledge, you proceed as a Magician (I), manipulating the inanimate world around you and finding out the boundaries.

Soon you realize that there are other kinds of knowing, and as a High Priestess (II), you start freeing your intuition. This doesn't prove to be enough, and you find that everything in nature has to be in balance, and through the mother stereotype, the Empress (III), you explore your interest in nature, life and creation, and start to listen to the emotional world. Now you know enough about your environment and become aware that there is an internal structure to all things.

Through father stereotype, Emperor (IV), you discover authority and rules. Finally, you become interested in other people and the mysteries of outer world and through Hierophant (V); you learn it's ways and beliefs and how to become a part of it. A need arises for a deeper connection with others – Lovers (VI) – but it proves difficult to find a balance between passion and reality.

You become aware of your value and you are no longer a child. With Chariot (VII), you take off alone into the wide world, decisive and self-confident, but you quickly begin to realize that having control isn't exactly easy and you are forced to develop discipline and willpower. Soon, you are forced to find your inner Strength (VIII) and to confront your first real problems and challenges, both in the outer world and, more importantly, in yourself.

This leads to a quest for answers and as a Hermit (IX) in isolation, you strive to understand all the whys and acquire a deeper understanding of yourself. You discover the connection of all things, and everything begins to "click."

Through the Wheel of Fortune (X), you accept fate as a legitimate factor in life and the whole universe, and it's exactly fate that unrolls the story further into the unexpected. You continue to better understand the whole picture and how your complete past creates the present.

Finally, through Justice (XI), you accept responsibility for your own life and realize that right now, your each and every tiniest action makes your future.

You have learned a lot but now you understand that you have just scratched the surface. You must learn to let go in order to proceed. As a Hanged Man (XII) you look at the world from a reversed perspective. You may be judged a fool by others, but you'll continue the journey unburdened and with much more solid foundations.

Transformation represented by Death (XIII) begins, and despite the great pain of the whole life phase ending, you are confident that you are on the right track and you leave a big part of your ego behind.

Finally, you develop a strong inner balance, and the wild wondering about your actions and motivations disappears. Through Temperance (XIV), you start to apply the newly discovered powers of moderation and flexibility.

You have come so far, nevertheless, you continue to explore your inner self, and through the Devil (XV), soon start very painful confrontations with your dark depths. You find the chains that constrain you from further growth in previously hidden areas of your ignorance, self-deceptions and addictions.

You free yourself of your chains and your misery only when you bring down your whole world represented as the Tower (XVI). Maybe only the external cataclysm gave you a huge enough impulse to finally act and free yourself; and however painful this process proves to be, your understanding is finally deep. You are getting somewhere.

The goal is finally clear as a Star (XVII), and it gives you hope and faith to continue on calmly. But it's not over yet; the last challenge is the Moon (XVIII) whose illusions seduce and confuse you so that you question what needs to be questioned and what doesn't until you learn to discern illusion from truth.

After the doubts and tricks of night, the Sun (XIX) brings the crystal clarity of the day; which you go through with great confidence and knowledge of yourself.

Finally, you stop and take inventory of all that is behind you (Judgment (XX)). However hard won your experiences have been, you rise above your ego, your shortcomings and your limitations, and you are ready for next level of existence.

You have learned all the lessons and successfully integrated all parts of yourself into a fully-complete and balanced whole. Through the World (XXI), you reach a new level of happiness and fulfillment.

However, although this cycle has concluded, you are ready for a new journey on a completely new level.

Here's How to Memorize the Major Arcana Cards

It was easy and fun, wasn't it? Now let's try to summarize together the cards' lessons briefly.

0. The Fool – Clean slate

I. The Magician – Learning about external world

II. The High Priestess – Acknowledging your intuition

III. The Empress – Integrating your female powers

IV. The Emperor – Integrating your male powers

V. The Hierophant – Learning the rules of the outer world

VI. The Lovers – Need for others

VII. The Chariot – Go into the world

VIII. Strength – Trials uncover your strengths

IX. The Hermit – Stop to re-think what you have learned

X. Wheel of Fortune – Accept there are things you can't control

XI. Justice – Learn to take responsibility

XII. The Hanged Man – New perspective

XIII. Death – Painful change

XIV. Temperance – Moderation can be a tool

XV. The Devil – Confronting your own demons

XVI. The Tower – Start over

XVII. The Star – Goal and hope

XVIII. The Moon – More than meets the eye

XIX. The Sun – Power and clarity

XX. Judgment – Leave the past behind

XXI. The World – Fulfillment and completeness

Don't worry about the above summary being over-simplified. We are simply using it for the progression to "stick" easier. Your mind will fill in the rest.

If you are actually trying to learn the cards (as opposed to reading this out of curiosity) try to tell the story to yourself now. Btw don't memorize the above summary; its main purpose was just to make you stop and think.

So just go through the cards again and tell a story. Don't worry if you can't remember all the meanings, simply have fun with it; improvise based on the card's picture and go on to the next card. Once when you have finished the whole story then check the cards you had problems with and then try again.

In this way you will learn all 22 Major Arcana cards in minutes, and not only their meanings but also their place in the big picture.

PS. Download the free companion e-book "Easy Tarot Reference: 78 Cards Explained"

One of the rewarding experiences in learning Tarot comes with a sense of wonder when reading the in-depth explanations for a single card that greatly interests you at the moment.

Maybe you haven't got a book included together with your deck. Or you simply want to read up more on the particular card.

No problem here. To make your experience more complete, I have put together another e-book: "Easy Tarot Reference: All 78 Cards Explained". You can regard it as a "companion" to this book, because:

1. It gives a perfectly traditional overview of all 78 Tarot cards
2. It's COMPLETELY FREE for you since you have purchased this book

Download it from the customer part of my website (just type below link in your web browser):

http://howtolearntarot.com/index.php/6-stories-bonus

Now that you have learned the Major Arcana cards and seen for yourself how easy and fun it can be, let's do the same with Minor Arcana (the four suits). We'll start with the suit of Swords.

Chapter 3. Swords Suite Represents Intellect and Conflict

Cold Rationality Often Leads to Trouble

Four suits are called Minor Arcana. They don't deal with your inner battles and personal growth. What they talk about are some specific everyday worries, events and emotions of yours.

Swords have two sides of the blades and represent the mind which solves complex problems but can also be a source of conflict and destruction and is to be used carefully. It is a great power that can be used for either good or ill.

Swords deal with cold rationality that often leads you to take uncompromising actions with courage. But the most brilliant mind can get into (or even provoke) a lot of trouble when not balanced by spirit and feeling.

If you have a deck at hand, look at the Swords cards. People on them surely look grand and admirable. But they don't look very happy, do they? Keep that in mind when going through the cards.

Now, let's memorize the story of the Swords. Again, you'll learn quicker and have more fun if you look at each card as you come to it.

The Story No.2: Struggle of the Swords

It has suddenly dawned on you how to resolve complex situations (Ace), and you are full of renewed energy as you start towards the solution.

Of course, you are quickly faced with a tough decision (2), and you are stuck because you don't know how to integrate two critical but contradicting interests.

Finally, you made the decision, and there is no going back. You move on, but the consequences are painful

(3) because, whatever you had to do, some options are now lost forever.

Maybe it's best to restrain from too much action (4), charge your batteries and prepare for the conflict that's coming.

The conflict came and went, and somehow you have won (5) but not without losses; you realize that each victory is at the same time someone else's defeat. Maybe you could have done better, but the path is clear now.

Finally, without distractions, but also without much joy (6), you continue along the path toward your goal. You have found out the hard way that your actions affect other people too.

But the path everyone expects you to take is not for you, and on your own, you go for the alternative (7).

As is often the case in life you got yourself into a tough situation with seemingly no way out (8). But there is both the solution and the path to take, if only you managed to open your eyes and see things as they really were.

You are in reach of your goal, but worries and doubts are killing you (9), and subconsciously you don't dare to take the last step. What you need is to find the courage to honestly confront your fears and expectations.

The situation is finally and conclusively resolved (10), and although the result may be far from what you hoped for, the long struggle is over. Unexpectedly, you feel almost calm ... now is the moment for reflection and learning your lessons.

Here's How to Memorize the Swords Cards

Let's quickly summarize each scene in the story. Think of a role each card plays as part of a progression:

Ace of Swords – Brilliant solution dawned on you

Two of Swords – Tough decision

Three of Swords – Some options are lost forever

Four of Swords – Prepare for conflict

Five of Swords – Bitter Victory

Six of Swords – Your actions affect others

Seven of Swords – Path others don't agree with

Eight of Swords – No way out

Nine of Swords – Doubts are killing you

Ten of Swords – Conclusive resolution

Again, don't memorize the above summary; it's just the tool to think about the cards.

Instead, try to tell the story by yourself. Use the cards and don't worry if you have to improvise. You'll typically need to do this only couple of times to memorize all the Swords.

Repeat it tomorrow (or when next gush of enthusiasm grabs you) and you'll be able to recall the cards for a long, long time.

Another thing you have probably noticed is that there are more Swords that I didn't mention yet: Page, Knight, Queen and King. These are called Court Cards and it's usually quite a challenge to understand them.

So I have given a whole chapter to the Court Cards with special "tricks" to help you both to understand and to memorize them. For those of you who wondered (and bothered counting), Court Cards are the sixth story from the title of this book.

Ok, now that you know the cards dealing with the rational mind, it's time to master the emotions and the Suit of Cups.

Chapter 4.
Suite of Cups
Represents Love and
Emotions

Advice on Love and Relationships

We already established that Cups represent your emotions; basically your love life and relationships with other people. Cups are related to the Water element so its actions are indirect but very powerful, and water always finds its way, just like emotions.

In other words, Cups are associated with anything emotional, from marriage to personal possessions and concerns. This also covers anything relating to partnerships, whether in a work or personal context. The actions influenced by the Cups are very different from, let's say, Swords direct-action approach.

Let's go through the story of the Cups suit. If your deck is at hand, take it out and put the Cups cards in front of you.

The Story No.3: Fulfillment of the Cups

Suddenly you recognize a new beginning; you feel it as (1) an emerging river of positive emotions and even though it's still small, you know nothing can stop it.

You let yourself be guided by your intuition, and you are rewarded with a deep emotional connection (2) full of the hope and promise that mutual enrichment will grow into real harmony and balance.

Your problems are behind you and fulfillment is here. You are happy (3) with what you now have and you are ready to enjoy even more good things that are bound to come.

You are surrounded by happiness but you feel there is more (4) and you don't enjoy it so much anymore; you start taking what makes you happy for granted.

Soon, the feeling off fulfillment vanishes and you decide to move on. You mourn what could have been

(5) and are disappointed with both yourself and others.

The past comes back to help you (6) and again you gain inner harmony. Calm and confident, you are open once more to new experiences.

It's time for real effort and to cease building castles in the air (7). You realize that some of life's choices are not in reality what they had seemed.

You go through much happiness and sorrow to get what you have, but your happiness is only an illusion (8) and drains your life energy from you. You recognize the moment is here and leave stagnation behind you. You move on to the unknown.

Finally, you are in complete harmony with your intuition, and your goals and desires become crystal clear. You are so aware and confident that you radiate happiness (9), and create it both for yourself and the people around you.

After a long and hard journey, you remember everything you've been through and completely and consciously enjoy (10) your dreams coming true; because you know that complete awareness of everything that has led to this moment is the only way to reach for even more.

Here's How to Memorize the Cups Cards

Let's summarize in the same way as with Major Arcana and the Swords; look at each card and think about it's scene in the story.

Ace of Cups – New well of positive emotions

Two of Cups – Emotional connection

Three of Cups – Happy with accomplishment

Four of Cups – Taking it all for granted

Five of Cups – Moving on

Six of Cups – Memories bring help

Seven of Cups – Castles in the sky

Eight of Cups – Time to leave again

Nine of Cups – Success

Ten of Cups – Dreams coming true

You know the drill by now.

Use the cards to tell the story by yourself; improvise if needed. Repeat a few times to fill in the gaps and to make it stick. And don't forget to repeat again tomorrow.

Chapter 5.
Wands Suite
Represents Your
Passion and Drive

A Powerful Force but Hard to Control

Wands represent your spirit: your passions, your drive and your projects and hobbies.

Cards of the Wands suite are impulsive; a spark of inspiration that brings to the surface a powerful force but hard to control; like fire.

The Story No.4: Implementation of the Wands

Suddenly you are struck with a great idea (1) which has sparked your ambition and you are full of passion and energy to start implementing it.

As soon as you start, you are excited about the different possibilities (2). You stop to think about the big picture and to let your intuition tell you how to proceed.

You put everything in motion (3) and intensely monitor the events and how they are bringing you nearer to your goal.

Solid foundations are set, and you enjoy tangible results (4) but you know you can't revel in them for too long but must go on.

You are stuck in a conflict; you feel attacked from all sides (5). Others don't agree with your ideas on how to proceed and at the same time, you are not completely sure of the ethical implications of your actions.

You win and with all the support you need you go on (6); but you shouldn't enjoy the victory too early and had better take care to keep your focus.

Opposition confronts you (7); but despite your fears and doubts, you have to prevail. It's the moment to defend not only what you have achieved but also to defend what is yet to come.

The goal is near and the path is clear (8). Quick and resolute action is needed but you stop for a moment to prepare; you don't want to make a wrong move in haste.

You are almost in reach of your goal and you are very tired of everything (9) but now you know you have everything it takes to overcome any obstacle. You find the needed strength and willpower to defend your success from any unexpected last minute problem, even though it might seem almost impossible.

Finally, you reach your goal (10) but you are burned out and don't enjoy the whole picture. You are worried only about the results and can't see how they actually burden you. For too long you have taken all the responsibility on yourself; you mustn't keep your head in the sand any longer, and widen your perception again. It's time to take inventory of everything that has passed and continue with your life.

Here's How to Memorize the Wands Cards

Again think of the each card's role in the story:

Ace of Wands – Great idea

Two of Wands – Different Possibilities

Three of Wands – Plans are moving ahead

Four of Wands – Tangible results

Five of Wands – Attacked from all sides

Six of Wands – You win

Seven of Wands – Defend from opposition

Eight of Wands – Path is clear

Nine of Wands – Defend your success

Ten of Wands – Success is a burden

Now tell the story by yourself a few times, the same as with the other suits.

Notice that there is only one suite left, the Pentacles. We are already getting close to the real thing: reading the spreads by yourself.

Chapter 6. Pentacles Suite Represents Money and Material Matters

Material World: Get Down to Earth

Pentacles represent the Earth element and symbolize material (more "down to earth") matters. The first that comes to mind is money, but also physical manifestations of stability, caution and effort.

Remember that Pentacles, as any of the four Tarot suits, deal with everyday worries and concerns. For example, when Pentacles talk about great success, it indeed is great success; but that means great success in your current endeavor or in something you are now planning – not the early retirement with millions stashed in the bank. Well, except if that is exactly what your current project is about.

The Story No.5: The Hard Work of the Pentacles

Luck has smiled on you and a very practical opportunity presents itself (1). You are going for the realization of the opportunity but with no haste because you know that if you go step by step and carefully build strong foundations, then nothing can stop you.

Of course decisions and risks come quickly (2) and you are extremely busy. The only way to keep everything in balance is to go with the flow, keeping focused at the same time.

Soon, you have the first tangible results (3). People around you recognize your accomplishments and even the hard work you put in is fulfilling.

You have achieved much but you have become paranoid about keeping what you have (4). You have isolated yourself from everyone. You won't be fulfilled again until you learn to freely use the results of your efforts and continue further with no fear.

As soon as real problems arise your world falls apart (5). You have to somehow gather the last atoms of energy and faith to endure and finally to find a smarter way to keep going.

You stop being an island unto yourself; you have learned to accept help when needed and also to provide help for other people (6) and things are going well again.

You have done all you can for now and present success is evident; but you are restless and worry about how to proceed (7). However, you realize that some things can't be hastened; so you use the moment of rest to carefully plan your next steps.

You have chosen the way and it brings you totally new experiences (8). Life isn't easy now but you are determined and you know that through commitment and excellent work, you are getting closer to more permanent and complete success at the same time that you grow as a person.

Finally, you have everything and what is more, you have achieved great authority and balance (9). In fact, you have already succeeded no matter what happens next.

You have achieved everything you planned and have created strong foundations (10) that give you both the opportunity and the stability to start new cycles, not only for your gain but also for the people that surround you.

Here's How to Memorize the Pentacles Cards

Look at the each card and think of its place in the progression:

Ace of Pentacles – New opportunity

Two of Pentacles – Decisions and risks

Three of Pentacles – First tangible results

Four of Pentacles – Paranoid about keeping what you have

Five of Pentacles – Have faith and endure

Six of Pentacles – Accept and give help

Seven of Pentacles – Worry how to proceed

Eight of Pentacles – Apprentice

Nine of Pentacles – Authority and success

Ten of Pentacles – Strong foundations for everything

Don't fall into the trap of memorizing the above summary. Instead, tell the story yourself. It might take several tries to do it right, but remember that when you are stuck, just look at the card and improvise.

Btw this "improvising approach" is not meant to substitute for understanding the cards. What it does is improve your "feeling" for the cards, without breaking the story thread you are in fact memorizing.

And remember the Court Cards we mentioned earlier, representing the actual people and personalities? They are explained in the next chapter, as the final ingredient in learning the cards.

Ian Eshey

Chapter 7.
Court Cards
Represent Different
Personalities and the
Actual People

Tricky to Learn but Easy to Recognize

Court cards can be tricky to learn because each represents both conflict and the synergy between the card's suit and responsibilities of the card's rank.

You already know what each suit represents and the ranks, ie. positions, in the court family are:

Pages – Curious children that seek experience

Knights – Young action types

Queens – Wisdom and influence

Kings – Authority and control

What you need to understand is that Court Cards represent personalities. In a reading, they can point to actual people influencing you or to aspects of yourself that you need either more of or less of in particular situation.

The easiest way to learn the Court Cards is to find the person with that personality traits and characteristics. And there is a little trick here; since the Court Cards represent stereotypes, the perfect candidates are members of your family or famous celebrities and the like.

Note that the card's sex can be misleading: pages and knights can represent both males and females. On the other hand, Queens and Kings are so strong mature female/male stereotypes that it's quite rare for them.

The story I wrote about the Court Cards is a little different than the rest. I will show you what those stereotype personalities are and how they function. Your job is to try to find the actual person who matches that stereotype.

The Story No.6: Discussions of the Court Cards

It was business as usual in Tarot Cafe; guests were seated as usual and four animated discussions were taking place.

Pages

Occupants of the first table were four Pages, always hungry for the experience they generally lack and day-dreaming about new possibilities, as usual, because their youthful outlook gives them an unfailing spring of ideas.

As always, the Page of Wands, whose creativity is unmatched, speaks first. He is full of fire and ornately tells about his new, rather original idea, which has surprisingly big potential.

Next, it's the turn of the Page of Cups whose intuition guides him through the day telling the others how he made a deeper connection in a particular relationship and how he feels that his dreams will become reality.

Third, the Page of Swords speaks. He is perhaps the most balanced of all the Pages. He explains how he performed an unusually objective analysis of the situation and found a completely unexpected way of addressing the complex problem that has been bothering him lately.

The Page of Pentacles speaks last. Known to be the most responsible and down to earth of all, he explains how openness to new ideas has brought him to finally understand how to wisely use the resources available to take this particular opportunity that presented itself.

Knights

At the second table, four Knights are talking about their missions.

First, the Knight of Wands speaks. He has neither patience nor the inclination to beat around the bush and declares that he is starting right away and knows exactly how he will accomplish the task. He is extremely confident because it's just this combination of creativity and determination that has started and finished many difficult projects.

Next, the idealistic and romantic Knight of Cups speaks. He reads people better than any other Knight, and speaks of his indirect plan of achieving the goal; he might have to manipulate some people a bit but with no bad intentions.

Third, it is the fearless Knight of Sword's turn. He is totally without emotions and presents an unbiased analysis of the problem (like in a game of chess) and his direct solution; he is unconcerned that his approach potentially leads to a conflict.

Lastly, the Knight of Pentacles speaks. He is the most conservative and methodical of all and explains a very realistic and detailed plan of how to succeed in his mission, which needs much persistence and effort but simply can't fail.

Queens

At the third table four Queens are exploring some very complex situations, as usual, because their greatly valued advice and wisdom are needed. They have a knack of putting things in the right perspective.

First, the most ambitious one of all speaks – the Queen of Wands. She can indeed be a best friend but also a worst enemy. She tells how by putting the right ideas in the right ears, everything will come out as she wants.

Next, the Queen of Cups speaks tuning easily in on others emotions. Her intuition is great but her own lack of pragmatism will probably require someone else to put her ideas into action.

Third is the direct and truthful Queen of Swords who isn't exactly easy to be around. She speaks about her demands for perfection.

And the last to tell her story is the generous and sometimes too caring Queen of Pentacles whose wisdom provides for stability and the balance of the mundane and emotional. Nevertheless, she sometimes goes too far in trying to achieve total security for those she cares for.

Kings

As usual, at the fourth table, four Kings sit and plan how to organize new projects. Their authority, knowledge and experience motivate all the others and get things moving.

First is the born leader, the King of Wands. He always recognizes and draws the best from people. Almost like he is enjoying the complex challenge he explains, without single trace of doubt, how he will get the unique qualities of each of his men into synergy and implement the project.

Next, the born diplomat, the King of Cups, speaks. He never judges but also never shares his motives. He asks for tolerance and moderation and says that he always listens to everyone before he decides who will be actually be assigned to do something.

Third, the harsh but fair King of Swords speaks. He is a decisive and brilliant commander and presents a brilliant, as always, analysis of the problem and who will do what is necessary to resolve it.

And last is the most pedantic of all, the King of Pentacles. His thoroughness and belief in hard work are legendary. He tells of a plan to seize good opportunities, slowly but surely, through team work and well-defined responsibilities.

Here's How to Memorize the Court Cards

I believe you have matched many stereotypes to actual people you know right away.

Here is the summary that will help you further. This time I have grouped cards by their suit. Read the stereotypes and match more of the cards to real people. Use the cards to look at the pictures.

A suits characteristic is very pronounced in personality traits of the Court Cards.

Wands are creative and adventurous; spontaneity and a lot of action make them very charismatic:

Page of Wands – Free-spirit, adventurous youth with endless source of new ideas he wants to try.

Knight of Wands – A living embodiment of daring and enthusiasm.

Queen of Wands – Very results-oriented lady; better don't get in her way.

King of Wands – Natural born leader of people; very charismatic.

Cups are empathic; they are extremely good at reading people. They tend to be dreamers, very intuitive but not very pragmatic

Page of Cups – A dreamer, a sensitive and emotional artistic type.

Knight of Cups – Chivalrous romantic; the true knight in shining armor.

Queen of Cups – Beautiful and caring; a mother figure.

King of Cups – A visionary and born diplomat.

Swords are guided by dry logic, so they are usually perceived as brilliant but cold:

Page of Swords – Quick witted, intelligent youngster; quite defiant and rebellious.

Knight of Swords – Gallant hero, but actually quite self-seeking.

Queen of Swords – An "ice queen".

King of Swords – Born general; the supreme strategist.

Pentacles are conventional and very responsible; they are "slow but sure" achievers:

Page of Pentacles – Ambitious yet committed and responsible; an ideal student.

Knight of Pentacles – A methodical and diligent perfectionist.

Queen of Pentacles – Devoted and pragmatic; the ideal head of a household.

King of Pentacles – A master of material concerns; everything he touches turns to gold.

Chapter 8.
The Lazy Man's Way
to Perform Complete
Tarot Readings

3 Simple Rules Guarantee a Good Reading

Ok, you are reading this book to be able to read the cards (plural). Not to interpret a single card but to relate multiple cards in a reading to discover insights into a particular problem.

But what makes a good reading? Obviously a lot of things, but with time I have realized there are three absolute musts.

With experience you will find many guidelines that work for you. But keep these three rules in mind and you'll be perfectly fine, right from the start.

Rule No.1: Form the Most Productive Question

First you need a reasonable question. For example, the following question is not very productive: "Will I get a raise tomorrow at the meeting with my boss?"

Instead, consider the following for the same situation: "What are the advantages and obstacles? What should I focus on?"

It will get you much further in investigating your situation and the options available to you.

Actually, each card in a spread represents one aspect of your situation. So the above "sub-questions" would become the cards in a spread. A good overall theme (THE question) for that reading would be "How should I approach tomorrow's meeting?"

But let's get back to those sub-questions in the following rule.

Rule No.2 Finding a Meaningful Spread for a Particular Situation

After establishing the question, you open the cards in a spread. The Internet is full of different spreads, but each tries to point to different aspects of the situation you are interpreting.

It's perfectly ok to ask specific questions and open one card for each. For example, one card tells you the pros, and another the cons, of the situation.

Or two cards tell you the positive and negative sides of a decision you are considering. Or when you are considering two options, you can ask what you gain and what you lose for each.

At the beginning, the easiest spread to learn is to open three cards for the past, the present and the future of a given situation. And of course, nobody said you can't combine all of the above.

Rule No.3 Reading Is a Story

And finally you come to interpreting the cards.

I have already stated this several times: it's NOT simply about meanings of individual cards.

What matters maybe even more is how the cards are RELATED.

What is the position the card represents? Do you see a progression or a contrast in the cards or in the positions?

Sounds complicated, but there is an easy solution.

After you open the cards, open your perception wide and pay attention to your intuition. With a little practice, you will notice all that matters all by itself.

Your job is simply to listen.

Interpreting Particular Cards in a Reading

Major Arcana in a reading

Major Arcana cards point to big lessons in life. They represent something both important and lasting (for at least some time, that is), and the need for the maturation of a segment of the inner self.

The whole reading needs to be considered in the light of the lesson a Major Arcana card is teaching.

The more Major Arcana cards, the less control one has over the situation.

Minor Arcana in a reading

Minor Arcana cards fill in the mundane details; they tell you about some specific everyday worries, events and emotions.

Court Cards in a reading

For particular situations, Court cards can either point to other people influencing you or to aspects of yourself that you need either more of or less of.

Court cards are intriguing, they represent both conflict and the synergy of two forces: The card's basic nature (which of the four Tarot suits it belongs to) and traditional responsibilities of its position in the court hierarchy.

Positive and negative card implications

Don't forget that each card has both positive and negative implications.

A simple rule for when to focus on negative implications is

1. If we either open the card and it's reversed, or
2. A card is placed in a "negative" position in a spread.

A card coming up reversed is obvious but what is a negative position?

Let's say you use a spread with "Obstacles" as one of the spread's positions. That would mean you should focus on the negative here, obviously. All well and good, but what do you do if a seemingly completely positive card comes up: Ten of Pentacles, the Sun, or the World?

Then the key is in that precise word: "seemingly". Success can make you soft. The Sun can burn you. Balance can be an illusion.

Or it could be something entirely different. You get the picture.

Chapter 9. Putting it All Together: Examples of Real-Life Tarot Readings

And Now to The Cards

By now, you probably can't wait to open the cards. I know that I couldn't wait if I were you.

So let's do a few readings together.

First, I will show you the simple Tarot spread everybody just loves: the three card spread. It is the easiest spread to begin with. You put three cards in the positions for Past, Present and Future – and you have a story.

When reading cards for my friends, most often they want to gain insights about one of two things. Either a relationship issue they have or some financial situation. So I will show you also the example for both.

By the way, do you remember general reading "rules"?

Let's repeat them, just in case.

First, form the most productive question (it shouldn't be a "yes or no" question). Next, find a meaningful spread for a particular situation – what are the angles that need to be investigated. Then, make a story out of the position of each card in a spread. Let your intuition take charge.

Several more things to remember before we start:

Major arcana cards point to big lessons in life while minor arcana cards tell you about some specific everyday concerns.

Court cards can either point to other people influencing you – or to aspects of yourself.

If a card represents something negative, we simply focus on its negative implications. Sometimes, too much of a good thing can be bad, or things are simply not as they seem.

Ok, let's go.

Three Card Spread Example

As far as I can remember, I've been enjoying my vacations in our small family house at the coast. It hasn't been in good shape for years, and I've been playing with the idea of extensively redesigning both the interior and exterior. But in reality, I limited myself just to do the most needed repairs. Of course, a complete remodel would take a lot of money. But eventually I realized the money can't be the only reason why I'm so reluctant to do it.

So I decided to use the cards to investigate my deeper thoughts on this.

It would surely take some time to get to the bottom of this; my whole family is involved, so I was not at all sure I would be comfortable with what I might discover. But I had to start somewhere.

The simplest and safest thing was to do the three-card spread.

My question was simple and straightforward: "What are my real thoughts about this house?"

The three-card spread is one of the simplest, breaking the cards into:

1. The Past

1. The Present
2. The Future

The cards I opened were surprisingly to the point:

1. The Past: **King of Swords**
2. The Present: **Five of Pentacles**
3. The Future: **Nine of Pentacles**

The Past

The Present

The Future

A charismatic person from the past, and two pentacles representing the physical matters – house, family, finances. No surprise here.

Card 1: The past

King of Swords is a harsh but fair person, also being a decisive and brilliant commander. The cards obviously speak of my grandfather who built this house decades ago. (Actually he indeed was a high-ranking military officer, who even went to war). The house was in mint condition while he was in charge. And here actually lies the beginning of the problem. Last decade of his life or so (he died at age 88) he couldn't really keep up – but he wouldn't let anyone meddle in what he considered to be his responsibility, including this house.

Card 2: The Present

The current situation is represented by the **Five of Pentacles**. Everybody became paranoid about keeping what they have and isolated themselves from each other. This does sound like my family. But now the problem is here and nothing functions as it should. The key is not to quit but endure and find a smarter way of moving forward. Things won't improve until we all can both give and accept help from each other.

Card 3: The future

The future card is the **Nine of Pentacles**. After choosing a path and pursuing it with determination and commitment, great authority and balance is achieved. Success and great results are already here, whatever the final outcome proves to be.

In short, it seems there is no way out, nor any easy way toward results. Better to prepare myself for hard work that is coming.

But one thing was still bothering me: What should I specifically do? I decided to open one more card to clarify this point for myself. And the card I opened: **Ten of Swords**.

What should I do?

Great, two pentacles and two swords. Hard work, hard thinking, and conflicts.

But let's see what **Ten of Swords** tells me I should do.

After confronting fears and expectations, the situation is finally and conclusively resolved. Although the result may not be what I hoped for, I should calm myself and learn my lessons. The new cycle is about to begin.

Okay, so let's try to get the whole picture. The period of conflicts and of everyone looking only after themselves is about to end. The period of step-by-step continuous effort which will start is bound to bring great results. But what is needed right now is to make this transition somehow, to consciously end the current cycle and provide an impulse to start the next one. And taking action in this situation is much more important than worrying whether the action is the right one.

Love Reading Example

As I've said, my friends most often want insight about relationship issues or some financial situation. First, the love reading.

The Reading

My friend Dave recently started dating a girl named Mia. Things are going well and they are obviously very much attracted to each other, but they seem to be stuck at the very beginning. Dave has a feeling the emerging relationship doesn't go anywhere, but can't think of a reason why.

I haven't met Mia, but I've known Dave for years. I suggested a simple spread with cards helping us to decipher the following:

1. The obstacle that Dave perceives
2. The obstacle that Mia perceives
3. The important factor that Dave overlooked
4. What is the real issue?
5. The solution

Dave was very eager to start. This is what the cards showed:

1. The obstacle for Dave: **XX Judgment**
2. The obstacle for Mia: **Nine of Pentacles**
3. The important factor that he overlooked: **Three of Cups**
4. The real issue: **XVII The Star**
5. The solution: II The High Priestess

Obstacle for him

What he overlooked

The real issue

The solution

Obstacle for her

We immediately notice that we have three Major arcana cards, telling us the issue obviously has nothing to do with daily concerns. What we should focus on are major life choices and the journey we all take through life.

Card 1: The obstacle Dave sees is **XX Judgment**. Everything seemed (and was) fine and crystal clear. But now there is one thing stopping things from progressing to the next level, and that is integrating all the lessons learned and rising above one's ego.

Card 2: The obstacle Mia sees is represented by **Nine of Pentacles**. Mia doesn't have the stability she craves. But her goal is near. She invested much effort in it, and she might be even too focused. In fact, Mia doesn't need distractions right now.

Card 3: The surprise for Dave comes with **Three of Cups**. What he has overlooked is that they have much already, at this very moment. He and Mia have real emotional connection and are in balance. He obviously wants more, but maybe what they already have is the best they can have at the moment. They shouldn't take it for granted, but they should enjoy what they have right now. It seems pretty good under the circumstances; otherwise he wouldn't want to keep the relationship going.

This got Dave thinking. "Bizarre," he actually said, seeming just a bit frustrated, "But we might be onto something."

Card 4: We pressed on. The real issue is represented by **XVII The Star**. Both Dave and Mia started a new period of their lives, more free and true to themselves.Starting this new period means they both have a clear path in front of them. Hopes are high. But is it the same path for both? Is Dave sure his goal is real? It's quite possible their goals are different. In any case, Dave should avoid false hopes and really try to differentiate the truth from illusions.

Card 5: And the solution card, **II The High Priestess**? BothDave and Mia have learned to manipulate the external world and get results. But they must not do this now, especially not to manipulate each other. They should both listen more to their intuition and learn to trust their feelings instead of cold analysis and calculation. And this is only the prerequisite to coming to terms with one's emotions, which is still in the future.

To summarize what the cards seem to be saying to Dave: Don't calculate – go with the flow. Be true to yourself and ready to tell the truth from illusion. And relax. Don't create great expectations for the future – instead just enjoy the present.

Dave got quiet towards the end. When we started, he was curious and expectant. But now he was calm and deep in thought. "Good," I said to myself, "The cogs are spinning; there is no doubt about that."

Notes on this reading

First we had to come up with questions that were relevant to the problem, in order to get usable insight. When the query is a concrete problem, it's useful to have one card pointing to something that is overlooked and another pointing to the real issue underneath.

When we opened the spread, I noticed that three of five cards were Major arcana.

This suggests the problem lies in life's greater lessons as taught by the Major arcana.

In this spread, we have three cards representing something negative, like a problem. When reading these particular cards, we look for their negative implications. Maybe we lack the main theme represented by the card, or we are too focused on something. Sometimes, too much of a good thing can be bad, or things are simply not as they seem.

Summary

Reading the cards really got Dave thinking, not about what the cards said, but about what Dave heard. His subconscious filtered the story so Dave recognized new lines of thought. They resonated so true that Dave couldn't help but start analyzing the situation from those new angles right away.

You can do that, too.

Follow your intuition and let the story unfold. Do it together with the person you are reading for. You are not doing an exercise in creative storytelling. You are helping another person to get in touch with his or her own subconscious knowledge of the situation.

And remember, each card is part of a progression.

Cards represent a story told by each suite. So for each card in a spread, think of a situation (i.e. card) that was before, and of a situation that comes after this particular card. In this way, you will have much greater context for the associations triggered by each card.

Reading tarot cards is as simple as that.

Career Reading Example

My friend Noelle asked me if she should change careers. She had been considering a particular career for quite some time, and just recently her boyfriend had surprised her. He suggested they take the required course for this new career together, and she wondered whether this was a sign.

I considered for a minute which questions would bring her new insights on this matter and chose the "fork-style" spread.

Laying out the Cards

Base of the fork:

1. Current situation
2. What she needs to know

First path:
3. Rational factors for change
4. Emotional factors for change
5. Consequences if she does change careers

Second path:

6. Rational factors against change
7. Emotional factors against change
8. Consequences if Noelle continues with her current job

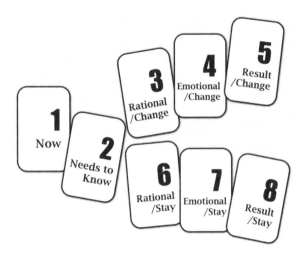

The Reading

Noelle was thrilled with this approach, so I opened the cards. This is what the cards showed for each position in a spread:

1. Current situation: **King of Pentacles**
2. What she needs to know: **VI The Lovers**

"Change career" path:

3. Rational factors: **Five of Swords**
4. Emotional factor: **King of Wands**
5. Consequences: **XXI The World**

"Stay on this job" path:

6. Rational factors: **Four of Pentacles**
7. Emotional factors: **XIV Temperance**
8. Consequences: **Ten of Cups**

Rational (change)   Emotional (change)   Result (change)

Current situation

What she should know

Rational (stay)   Emotional (stay)   Result (stay)

"It's never boring for you," I half-teased her. "Even when changing careers, what you are really thinking about are two men: the current secure one and the future passionate one." Noelle just smiled and gave me a neutral comment, along with a meaningful what-can-I-do look.

What we can immediately see from the cards is that this is no simple "financial" issue. We have two Major arcana cards, along with multiple cups and pentacles. Important life lessons, money, and emotions are all intertwined, both in the present moment, and on both paths.

The two kings are important, of course, safety now and possible passion in the future. And another, perhaps the most important angle, is that both paths lead to improvement and doing well. Both lead to different kinds of improvement and to different good things. Both outcomes are good.

Card 1: Current situation

King of Pentacles has great influence on Noelle's current situation. And it doesn't seem purely financial. Yes, the question is "material," and yes, this card is Pentacles. But everything here seems related to everything else. And this King is the person who in some way provides Noelle with safety and security, which suspiciously sounds like her current boyfriend.

With the King of Pentacles, steady step-by-step success in the material world is almost guaranteed. However, this is not a quick process; rather it comes through hard work over time.

Card 2: What Noelle needs to know

What Noelle needs to be aware of is represented by the Major arcana card **VI The Lovers**. She has learned the workings of the world and how to be a part of it. What she now seeks is a deeper connection, a meaningful relationship perhaps. But she has yet to find a balance between her inner passions and reality.

Only when she finds that balance will she stop considering herself a child and build self-confidence and independence.

Now, let's examine the "career change" path.

Card 3: Rational factors for career change

Rational reasons for changing careers are symbolized by the **Five of Swords**. Noelle expected a conflict somehow related to this, and when the conflict came, Noelle won, but not without losses. Now she realizes that every victory is someone else's defeat. But the path is clear and Noelle can continue without distraction, although she won't have as much enthusiasm as before for this goal.

Card 4: Emotional factors for career change

Emotional factors influencing this path are represented by the **King of Wands**, a person led by his passions, but at the same time in control, both of himself and dominating others. This person can be somebody Noelle already knows (even herself, but she shakes her head to that), but also someone she hopes to meet.

I had begun to feel unsure for a moment, like I was "invading" in dubious matters, but Noelle encouraged me to go on. She then told me she is indeed looking for a serious relationship, and is unsure of the future of her current one. Noelle even considered that the reason for her wish for a career change could be to separate herself from the environment in which she met her current boyfriend.

I couldn't help but remember the conflict (the rational reason) and Noelle's own words that her boyfriend unexpectedly suggested they change careers together just days before. But I kept my mouth shut. It was for her to make connections and find deeper meanings.

The very real and human story seemed to start unfolding.

Card 5: Consequences of taking this path

The best thing was the **XXI The World**, which means a great life lesson and completing oneself into a balanced whole. Should she succeed in rising above her own ego and her own limitations, Noelle will reach happiness and fulfillment and be ready to journey through life on a completely new level.

Shifting gears, we read the rest of the cards and see the alternative, in other words the leave-things-as-they-are path.

Card 6: Rational factors against the change

Rational factors influencing the status quo are the **Four of Pentacles**. Noelle had worked hard and achieved much. But she wasn't fulfilled and became paranoid about keeping what she has. She even started isolating herself from others. As soon as real problems arose, everything would fall apart.

Note that the Pentacles represent the material world, but this doesn't necessarily mean money. It could mean home and family, which may mean that continuing down this road worries her. Maybe she could find herself dependent on being together with her boyfriend. Again, this was a long shot, which I don't usually do. But I learned to go with my strong feelings.

Noelle shot me a glance and wanted to comment, but cut herself short. This confirmed my suspicions, and we didn't need to investigate any further.

Card 7: Emotional factors against the change

Emotional reasons are **XIV Temperance**. After opening a new page in her life, despite great pains, Noelle found herself on the right track. She had started to apply newly discovered powers of moderation and flexibility and will continue to explore her inner self and some dark confrontations still awaiting her. But she is fully aware she has achieved much. She is in no hurry now, especially through some radical (at least for her) turns.

Card 8: Consequences of keeping status quo

And the result of pursuing the current path is the **Ten of Cups**. After Noelle's goals and desires become crystal clear to her, her own confidence will create happiness, both for herself and the people around her. She will be aware of everything she's been through, so she will be able to completely and consciously enjoy her dreams coming true. Again, a happy ending. Note that this is a spectacular result, but in "mundane" things (minor arcana), while the alternative path brings spectacular results (Major arcane) in self-growth and fulfillment.

Indeed, the cards have told an interesting story. Let's summarize.

The good news is that Noelle can't really make a wrong choice here. Both paths bring their own rewards. From the current promise of safety she either goes on a long journey with a life-changing new career, or continues to gradually build her success in her current situation. The long journey of change brings her inner growth and fulfillment, while pursuing the current path slowly but surely brings balance and happiness in everyday things.

In short, to me it sounds like "inner happiness" versus "outer happiness." Of course, the choice is hers to make. And remember that results are not mutually exclusive. They simply represent where the focus will be in the period to come. Luckily, my role was not to advise her, but to help her connect to her deeper thoughts on the matter.

Summary

Noelle had several insights, so reading the cards really got her thinking. Just as it was for Dave, Noelle's reading was not about what the cards said, but what she connected to. Her subconscious filtered the story, so she found new (and some of them disturbing) lines of thought.

You can do readings like this too. Follow your intuition and let the story unfold.

Thank You for Reading

Believe it or not, now you are perfectly capable of doing Tarot readings yourself.

The stories made you learn the cards in a way you won't forget. You have learned the symbols that are most often used in Tarot decks. The only thing left is to actually take the cards.

Follow your intuition and let the story unfold.

Do it together with the person you are reading for. You are not doing an exercise in creative storytelling. You are helping another person to come in touch with his or her own subconscious knowledge of the situation.

Remember this: individual cards do not tell much by themselves; each card is part of a story.

And thank you for reading. I hope this book will help you to have fun with Tarot and enjoy it as much as I do.

If you enjoyed this book, **please consider writing a short review** on Amazon or iBooks or another store you purchased it from. It would help this book to reach more people, and it would help other people to know what to expect.

About any feedback or comments you surely have, I'd sincerely like to hear them! You can reach me through my website:

http://www.HowToLearnTarot.com

Another way is to email me directly. The address is ian@howtolearntarot.com, but kindly be aware that I simply can't answer all the emails I get.

Take care,

Ian Eshey, July 2013

"Tarot Spreads for Love, Career and More: Get Your Questions Answered" by Ian Eshey

Available from Amazon.com and other book stores.

"Conversational, friendly, and fun, makes this book accessible to all levels of readers."

Despite what you may have heard about tarot reading, you don't have to be psychic to do one. There are a few simple things you need to know to start doing readings for yourself and your friends in no time.

This book includes spreads that answer a variety of useful questions:
- Simple spreads for beginners, including the one- and two- card spreads.
- Popular spreads like Horseshoe and Celtic cross.
- More specific spreads like "Does he love me?" and "How to get my ex back".

Spreads are easy to accomplish and include helpful pictures to give people more of an idea of what to focus on.

But this book is not only about spreads, it provides great advice with EXPLANATIONS AND EXAMPLES that show how something should be done and clarify what many people might have been doing wrong; e.g. framing questions correctly.

Stories in the book are very relatable and show real people; how they are often not even aware of small items that actually create their problems. And the real life sample readings tie together everything that has been said.

There is a free bonus to get less-experienced readers started; simple explanations of the cards and what they stand for as a free download from the website.

What other Tarot readers say about this book:

"I really liked the book. You explain the layouts and how to tweak them very well and make it sound fun and simple."

"A really well written book that lays out a wonderful starting method with clear explanations."

"An excellent book for anyone curious about tarot cards to pick up."

"I love that you make this simple enough that someone who is just starting can easily create a spread."

Just to give you a taste, here's the Table of Contents.

How to Make Money from Home
How to Find a Job

Chapter 6: Self-Improvement Spreads
Work-Life Balance
How to Deal With Stress
How to Be Happy

Chapter 7: Putting it All Together – Real-Life Example Readings
3-Card Spread Example
Love Reading Example
Career Reading Example
Celtic Cross Reading Example
Horse Shoe Spread Example

Available from Amazon.com and other book stores.